Air Fryer Cookbook for Beginners (UK)

1000-Day Quick, Tasty and No-Stress Air Fryer Recipes with Pictures
using European Measurements to Enjoy a Healthy and Happy Life.

Chieffy Linda

Table of Contents

INTRODUCTION

An air fryer is one of the most versatile cooking appliances which can be used to cook a variety of foods in a single appliance. It allows you to air fry, roast, bake, grill, reheat, and dehydrate your favourite foods. One of the best reasons to use an air fryer is that it requires less fat or oil to cook your food. The air fryer uses 80 to 85 percent fewer fats and oils compared to other traditional cooking methods. It reduces calories, fats, and the formation of harmful compounds during the cooking process. If you like fried food then an air fryer is one of the healthier cooking methods for frying food with the texture and taste of deep-fried food. Using an air fryer you can make your favourite snacks using less fats and oils. Air-fried food is one of the best alternatives to unhealthy traditionally fried food.

The air fryer works on rapid heat circulation technology to cook healthy and delicious foods. The heating element produces heat and blows this heat into the cooking chamber with the help of a convection fan to achieve even cooking results.

This cookbook contains healthy and delicious air fryer recipes from breakfast to dessertsand they are both unique and healthy. Each recipe begins with its preparation and cooking time followed by a full ingredients list and step-by-step cooking instructions. Each of the recipes end with their nutritional value information, which helps keep track of daily calorie consumption. There are lots of cookbooks available on the market on this topic so thank you for choosing my book. I hope you love and enjoy all the recipes contained in this cookbook.

What is an air fryer?

An air fryer is one of the most advanced and versatile kitchen appliances used to cook healthy and nutritious food. It fries your favourite food by circulating hot air into and through the cooking basket; it works on a rapid hot air circulation technique, whereby hot air is circulated into and through the food basket with the help of a convection fan which results in perfectly cooked foods. Compared with conventional cooking, an air fryer cooks your food faster and it is evenly cooked on all sides. An air fryer is a versatile cooking appliance capable of cooking a wide variety of foods. It makes your food crispier on the outside and juicy and tender on the inside. You are able to enjoy your favourite fried foods without the worry of extra fats and calories, which are harmful to a healthy lifestyle. Air fryers come in small and compact sizes and easily fit on your kitchen worktop.

Structure of the air fryer

1. Heating elements: The heating elements are in the top section of the air fryer. They produce the heat for cooking the food. Most advanced air fryers are thermostatically controlled and automatically turn the heating elements off when the desired temperature for cooking the food is reached.

2. Fan: The air fryer uses a fan to circulate hot air into the cooking chamber, similar to a convection oven, and it is evenly distributed around the food in the food basket. This helps to cook your favourite food more evenly and give crispier results.

3. Cooking chamber: The cooking chamber is situated below the heating element and convection fan. Most air fryers come with a non-stick coating. The chamber holds the food basket or food tray depending on the model of the air fryer.

4. Exhaust system: The air fryer exhaust system helps to filter the extra air present in the cooking chamber before releasing the smell of the food when it is cooked.

5. Cooling system: The cooling fan of the air fryer is situated at the top of the air fryer which helps to control the inner temperature of the air fryer. After it has finished cooking, the fan ensures that the inner part of the air fryer remains cool.

Food basket or food tray: The food basket is used to hold the food during the cooking process. Most air fryer baskets come with a food separator or tiers that allow the cooking of several types of foods at once.

Air frying step-by-step guide

If you are new to air frying, then the following step-by-step guide will help you to make healthy and delicious air frying recipes in no time.

1. Prepare your food: Food preparation saves your washing, slicing, peeling, mixing, grinding, cutting, and cooking time. Food goes through various stages before the cooking process begins. It also allows you to manage your portion sizes.

2. Prepare your air fryer food basket or tray: Before starting the cooking process always grease your food basket using cooking spray. Make sure all the sides and bottom are greased properly before placing food into the food basket. It helps to prevent food from sticking and makes cleaning easier.

3. Set temperature: Air fryers have preheat settings to enable preheating for 3 to 5 minutes before starting the actual cooking process. If your air fryer does not have a preheat function, then the temperature can be set manually to preheat the air fryer for 3 to 5 minutes before starting to

cook. There are different times and temperature settings for different foods. If foods are in smaller pieces these will cook quicker than large pieces of food.

4. Preheat your air fryer: Preheating is one of the essential processes to ensure quick and even cooking results. It also helps to save your cooking time and makes your food crispier. Generally, 3 minutes is sufficient for preheating your air fryer but a large-size air fryer my need around 5 minutes.

5. Place your food into the food basket: Arrange food pieces in the food basket and make sure there is a space between each piece of food. Don't overcrowd the food basket as it may give uneven results. If you are cooking two different food items at the same time then a food separator should be used. If a larger quantity of food is needed, then it should be cooked in batches.

6. Set cooking time: Set the cooking time using control panel functions as per your recipe needs. If you are not sure about cooking time, then set a shorter time first and slowly increase the time until your food is perfectly cooked.

7. Start the cooking process: After the time is set, press the start button and an LED light indicates the cooking process is started. Most advanced air fryers also include a pause button to temporarily interrupt the cooking process.

8. Flip or shake food: Flip or shake the food in the food basket when halfway through cooking time. This will help to cook your food evenly on both sides.

9. Remove food basket: When the timer reaches zero, remove the food basket using heatproof mitts or gloves. Now your food is ready to serve.

Benefits of air fryer

Air frying is one of the healthiest ways to cook your favourite foods. An air fryer comes with various benefits. Some of the most important include:

1. **Even Cooking:** The air fryer works on rapid air circulation techniques to cook your food faster and evenly. Hot air is circulated through the cooking chamber with the help of a fan. The heat is evenly distributed through the cooking chamber giving even and rapid results. It also adds a nice texture, making food crispier.

2. **Healthier choice:** Frying your food in an air fryer requires less fat and oil compared with deep frying. Using less fat and oil helps to reduce calorie intake by 70 to 80 percent. Air frying also cuts down the harmful compounds that can becreated during frying. If you like fried food but are worried about extra calorie consumption, then an air fryer is one of the healthiest choices. When deep-frying starchy foods, a harmful compound called acrylamide is created, which may increase the chances of getting cancer. In air frying, 90 percent less acrylamide is created than in deep-frying.

3. **Retains nutritional values:** When deep-frying most of the nutritional content of food is lost. The air fryer works on rapid air circulation requiring less fat and oil. .

4. **Multifunctional cooking appliances:** Most advanced air fryers provide multifunctional cooking options. They are capable of air frying, baking, roasting, keeping warm, grilling, reheating and dehydrating, depending upon the model you choose.

5. **Crispy and crunchy results:** Air fryers not only cook your food faster but also give a nice golden-brown texture to food. They make food crispier on the outside while remaining juicy and tender on the inside. This is because when high heat constantly circulates through the food basket it triggers a chemical reaction known as the Maillard reaction, which occurs due to a chemical reaction between the sugars and amino acids present in the food; this is what gives the food its delicious crispy golden-brown appearance and texture.

6. **Easy to use:** Air fryers do not need any special skill so anyone can easily

operate them. All the cooking functions are displayed on the control panel giving you the ability to choose the cooking function as per the recipe. Most of the functions are pre-programmed, which means you never need to worry about time and temperature settings. Put the food basket into the air fryer, select the appropriate function and press the start button. Time and temperature can be set manually as per the recipe.

7.Safe cooking appliance: The air fryer comes with overheating protection and is dishwasher safe, making cleaning smooth and easy. Most air fryers automatically shut down for safety reasons when the timer reaches zero. Air fryers are enclosed from all sides so there is no risk of splashing, spilling, or accidentally touching hot oil.

8.Promotes weight loss: Deep-fried foods are very high in calories and also high in unhealthy fats and oils. Intake of such unhealthy foods increases the risk of obesity. Air fryers cook food by using fewer fats and oils, and this means fewer calories are consumed, which promotes weight loss.

How to choose the right air fryer?

To choose the right air fryer various important key factors need to be taken into consideration.

1.Air fryer size and capacity

The air fryer size and capacity depends upon the available countertop space and the number of family members. Generally, air fryers are available in four different sizes.

I.Small size air fryer: Around 1 to 3 litre capacity, capable of cooking small and large batches of food such as snacks, chicken breasts, chicken wings, and more. These air fryers are ideal for a small family of 1 to 2 people.

II.Medium-size air fryer: Around 3.7 to 4.1 litre capacity, capable of cooking a medium and large quantity of food in a single cooking cycle. These air fryers are ideal for 3 to 6 family members.

III.Large-size air fryer: A large-size air fryer has a capacity of around 5.3 to 6 litre. These air fryers can cook multiple foods at the same time in a single cooking cycle. These air fryers are ideal for a family of 5 to 6.

IV.Extra-Large size air fryer: Extra-large size air fryers have a capacity of around 6 to 16-litres. Using these air fryers you can bake, roast, grill, and dehydrate large quantities of food. These air fryers are ideal for large families.

2.Temperature Control

Temperature controls play an important role in cooking results. The foods cooked at high temperature settings give faster and more even cooking results. Most foods like chicken and meat require about 200°C temperature forperfect results. To simplify the cooking process always choose an air fryer that comes with a temperature display and light indicators.

3.Power wattage

Power wattage is the consumption of electricity used in performing different cooking tasks. The higher-wattage air fryergives you better and faster cooking outcomes but they also consume more electricity. The most common air fryers are between the 800 and 2200 watts range. An air fryer of approximately 1500 watts is sufficient for a smooth cooking experience.

4.Preset functions:

It is a good idea to choose an air fryer that come with lots of useful preset or pre-programmed functions that set time and temperature for cooking everyday items.. These preset functions make your daily cooking process easy and faster.

5.Easy to use and to clean

The air fryer comes with two types of control panel systems one is the analogue control system and the other is the digital touch panel control system. Choose an air fryer that most suits your style of cooking and is convenient.

To make the daily cleaning process easy and simple always chooses a nonstick coated food basket to make the daily cleaning easy. The food basket is also easily removable and many are dishwasher-safe for easy cleaning.

6.Safety Features

Choose an air fryer that comes with a well-insulated handgrip to pick it up safely, because air fryers become extremely hot during cooking. Ensure your air fryer is equipped with an automatic shutdown program that shuts off your air fryer when cooking timer reaches zero. An air fryer that comes complete with overheating protection is better for safety reasons.

Tips and Tricks

1. Grease air fryer food basket: Grease your air fryer food basket using oil spray on the side and bottom of the basket. This will help to prevent food sticking to the food basket.

2. Avoid overcrowding: Always leave some space between food pieces because the air fryer cooks your food by circulating hot air around the food in the basket. If the basket is overcrowded this affects the cooking process and will result in uneven cooking.

3. Spray cooking oil over food halfway through cooking: When half the cooking cycle is completed spray a little cooking oil over your food to add extra crispiness to food.

4. Preheat air fryer: Always preheat your air fryer for 3 to 5 minutes before placing your food into the air fryer. Preheating not only saves your cooking time but also gives more even and crispier results.

5. Cook food in batches: Instead of overcrowding food in the baskets, it is better to cook food in batches to achieve the desired results.

6. Shake the air fryer basket halfway through cooking: Shake the air fryer basket when half of the cooking time has elapsed to achieve even cooking results.

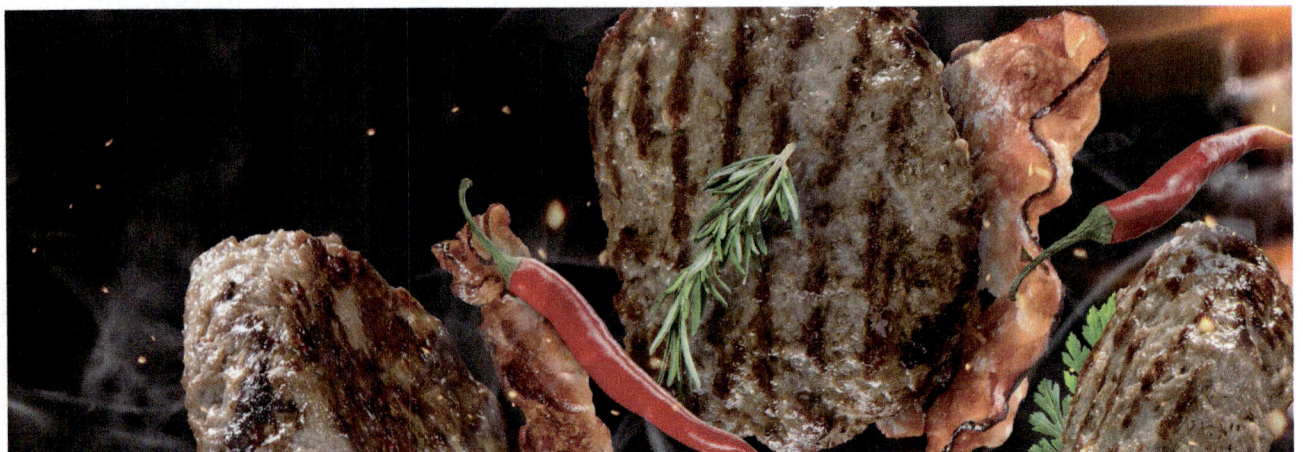

7. **Use an air fryer to reheat your leftovers:** If you use a microwave oven to reheat your leftovers it makes your food soggy. If you use an air fryer to reheat your leftovers you will get a crispier result.

8. **Do not use harsh chemicals when cleaning the food basket:** The food basket comes with non-stick coatings so it is advisable not not to use any harsh chemicals or abrasives for cleaning as these may cause damage to the nonstick coating.

9. **Do not sprinkle dry spices over food:** Spray food with a little oil before sprinkling with any dry spices. The oil holds the spices on the food during the cooking process. Without oil, it may blow out of the air fryer.

10. **While baking use parchment paper liners:** While baking use parchment paper liners to avoid cookies and cakes sticking. Parchment liner paper does not restrict the airflow.

11. **Drying the air fryer after cleaning:** Replace all of the washed parts in the air fryer and then run the air fryer for 2 to 3 minutes to allow everything to dry properly.

12. **For hygiene:** Make sure you clean the air fryer after every use as per the cleaning instructions given in the user manual. This will help to keep the air fryer hygienically clean.

13. **Prevent white smoke while cooking:** When cooking high-fat foods, like bacon, the dripping fat can cause the air fryer to emit white smoke into the air. To prevent this happening, just add some water to the bottom of the air fryer basket when cooking these high-fat foods.

Chapter 1: Breakfast

Air Fryer Frozen Sausage Rolls

Prep Time: 1 Minute
Cook Time: 18-20 Minutes (10-12 Minutes
   for Mini Sausage Rolls)   Serves: 4

Ingredients:

- 4 Large Frozen Sausage Rolls (or 12 Mini Sausage Rolls)
- 1 beaten Egg or some Milk for brushing

Directions:

1. Preheat the air fryer to 180°C.
2. Lay the frozen sausage rolls in the air fryer basket, allowing a bit of space between each one. Optionally brush with some beaten egg or milk. This will help turn the pastry golden.
3. Air fry large sausage rolls for 18 to 20 minutes, and mini sausage rolls for 10 to 12 minutes. Check on the sausage rolls at the halfway mark to ensure they are not burning.
4. At the end of the cooking time, the sausage rolls should be golden brown on the outside and piping hot on the inside. If the pastry is still pale, turn the air fryer temperature up to 200°C for 1 to 2 minutes.
5. Leave to rest for a few minutes before eating.

Nutritional Value (Amount per Serving):

Calories: 130; Fat: 9.31; Carb: 3.99; Protein: 9.28

Air Fryer Roast Potatoes

Prep Time: 5 Minutes
Cook Time: 25-30 Minutes   Serves: 3

Ingredients:

- 1/2 tbsp Vegetable Oil
- Salt and Pepper   • 600g Potatoes

Directions:

1. Preheat the air fryer to 180°C.
2. Peel, wash and chop the potatoes.
3. Drizzle with the vegetable oil and season with salt and pepper.
4. Add to the air fryer basket.

5. Cook for 15 minutes at 180°C. Shake well.
6. If you're adding additional herbs, spices or seasonings now if the time to add these.
7. Cook for another 10 minutes at 180°C. Check. If required cook for a further 5 minutes.

Nutritional Value (Amount per Serving):

Calories: 180; Fat: 2.5; Carb: 36.43; Protein: 4.26

Air Fryer Mashed Potatoes

Prep Time: 5 Minutes
Cook Time: 20-25 Minutes   Serves: 3

Ingredients:

- 500 g Baby Potatoes (first early works too)
- 15 ml Olive Oil
- Salt and Pepper
- 20 g Butter
- 1 stalk Chives

Directions:

1. Wash and dry the potatoes.
2. Place the potatoes on a piece of tin foil
3. Cover with 15ml of olive oil, sprinkle generously with salt and pepper. Wrap the foil over the potatoes.
4. Air fry at 200°C for 20 minutes.
5. Once the time is up ensure that the potatoes are fork tender. If not cook for 3-5 minutes more.
6. Once the potatoes are cooked through remove and place in a bowl.
7. Add 20g of butter and mash until smooth.
8. Season with salt and pepper.
9. Chop a stalk of chives and scatter on the top.
10. If you're serving family style then smooth the top and dab 10g of butter on top to give a nice presentation.

Nutritional Value (Amount per Serving):

Calories: 427; Fat: 29.21; Carb: 37.18; Protein: 8.59

Air Fryer Cheese Biscuits

Prep Time: 4 Minutes
Cook Time: 8-10 Minutes   Serves: 6

Ingredients:

- 115 g Self-Raising Flour
- 55 g Butter or Margarine
- Pinch of Salt
- 35 g Grated Cheddar Cheese
- 75 ml Semi-Skimmed Milk

Directions:

1. Mix together the self-raising flour and butter.
2. Add a pinch of salt.
3. Add grated cheddar cheese.
4. Combine well.
5. Add the semi-skimmed milk and mix.
6. Divide the mixture into 6.
7. Line the air fryer basket with parchment paper.
8. Drop the mixture inside the air fryer basket.
9. Cook at 200°C for 8-10 minutes.

Nutritional Value (Amount per Serving):

Calories: 633; Fat: 36.13; Carb: 33.12; Protein: 43.12

Air Fryer Pizza Scrolls

Prep Time: 10 Minutes
Cook Time: 6-7 Minutes   Serves: 6

Ingredients:

- 1/2 portion Pizza Dough
- 2 portions Roasted Tomato Pizza Sauce
- 60 g Grated Mozzarella and Cheddar Mix
- Mixed Italian Herbs Basil and Oregano

Directions:

1. Roll out the pizza dough as thinly as possible.
2. Spread over the roasted tomato pizza sauce.
3. Add the grated cheddar.

4. Sprinkle on 1/2 of your herbs.
5. Roll up as tightly as possible (I find that using baking paper or cling film works well here)
6. Slice into 2.5cm slices.
7. Pop into the air fryer basket.
8. Air fry at 200°C for 6-7 minutes until golden brown.
9. Sprinkle over the remainder of the herbs when serving.

Nutritional Value (Amount per Serving):

Calories: 324; Fat: 11.27; Carb: 42.2; Protein: 9.79

Air Fryer Toast

Prep Time: 1 Minute
Cook Time: 3-4 Minutes   Serves: 4

Ingredients:

- Sliced bread (I normally use 4 slices of sourdough sliced white or brioche style bread for the tastiest results)

Directions:

1. Preheat the air fryer to 200°C for a couple of minutes.
2. Place the slices of bread into the air fryer basket. If you've got an air fryer oven with racks then use one of the lower racks to keep the bread away from the heating element.
3. The main aim is to ensure that you only have one layer of toast, to avoid blocking the air from flowing around the air fryer basket freely.
4. You don't need to use any olive oil, or spray oil, when making toast, like I might suggest with other air fryer recipes.
5. Cook for 3-4 minutes, turning once during the cooking time.
6. You may find that your air fryer distributes the air well enough not to really need to turn, but I like to ensure even cooking wherever I can! Especially as it just takes a few seconds with a pair of tongs.
7. Remove when golden brown. You can adjust the cooking time up or down based on your own preferred toasting. I like a medium – golden brown, which is what the cooking times in this recipe are based upon.

Nutritional Value (Amount per Serving):

Calories: 176; Fat: 7.43; Carb: 2.79; Protein: 24.28

Air Fryer Mashed Potato Balls

Prep Time: 5 Minutes
Cook Time: 16 Minutes   Serves: 2

Ingredients:

- 300g of Leftover Mashed Potato
- 1 Egg
- 50g Breadcrumbs (homemade or packet are fine. For a different texture consider using Panko breadcrumbs).
- Salt and Pepper

Directions:

1. Take your leftover mashed potatoes.
2. Whisk one egg in a bowl. Season with salt and pepper.
3. Measure your breadcrumbs into a separate bowl.
4. Use a small ice cream scoop, or two tablespoons to roll your leftover mashed potato into small balls. The smaller the better to avoid them breaking up!
5. Once rolled, dip the mashed potato balls into egg and then breadcrumbs.
6. Spray the air fryer basket with spray oil.
7. Add the mashed potato balls into the air fryer basket.
8. Cook at 200°C for 16 minutes. Check, and gently shake, at 5 minutes, then 10 minutes in, just to avoid the balls sticking to the bottom of the air fryer basket.
9. Serve with tomato ketchup and enjoy.

Nutritional Value (Amount per Serving):

Calories: 247; Fat: 5.46; Carb: 34.83; Protein: 9.17

Air Fryer Falafel

Prep Time: 10 Minutes
Cook Time: 35 Minutes   Serves: 20

Ingredients:

For Falafel
- 1/2 Medium Yellow Onion, cut into quarters
- 4 Cloves Garlic
- 5g Packed Parsley Leaves
- 5g Packed Coriander Leaves
- 2 x 400g cans Chickpeas, rinsed and drained
- 1 tsp Salt
- 1 tsp Baking Powder
- 1 tsp Dried Coriander
- 1/2 tsp Chilli Flakes

For Tahini Sauce
- 80g Tahini
- Juice of 1/2 a Lemon
- 3 tbsp Water, plus more as needed
- Pinch of Salt
- Pinch of Chilli Flakes

Directions:

1. In a food processor, pulse onion, garlic, parsley, and coriander until roughly chopped, scraping down sides as needed. Add drained chickpeas, salt, baking powder, coriander, cumin, and chilli flakes. Pulse again until chickpeas are mostly broken down with some chunks. You want to stop just before the mixture turns into a paste. Taste and adjust seasonings.
2. Scoop out about 2 tablespoons worth of mixture and gently form into a ball without squeezing together too much or falafels will be dense. Working in batches, place falafels in air fryer basket and cook at 190°C for 15 minutes.
3. Meanwhile, make tahini sauce: In a medium bowl, combine tahini and lemon juice. Add water and stir until combined. Add more water 1 tablespoon at a time until desired consistency is reached. Season with a big pinch of salt and a pinch of chilli flakes.
4. Serve falafels with sauce, in a salad, or in a pitta.

Nutritional Value (Amount per Serving):

Calories: 36; Fat: 2.92; Carb: 1.88; Protein: 1

Chapter 2: Vegetables

Air Fryer Parsnips

Prep Time: 5 Minutes
Cook Time: 15 Minutes   Serves: 4

Ingredients:

- 4 Medium Parsnips
- 1 tbsp Oil
- Salt and Pepper to taste

Directions:

1. Top and tail the parsnips. Optionally peel the parsnips.
2. Drizzle oil over the parsnips and toss until they are covered.
3. Season with salt and pepper according to taste.
4. Transfer the parsnips to the air fryer basket.
5. Set the temperature to 200°C and air fry for 15 minutes.
6. Shake the air fryer basket at the halfway mark.
7. The parsnips will be soft in the middle and golden brown on the outside when they are ready, if not, air fry for a little longer.

Nutritional Value (Amount per Serving):

Calories: 107; Fat: 3.88; Carb: 16.49; Protein: 3.31

Air Fryer Brussels Sprouts

Prep Time: 10 Minutes
Cook Time: 15-20 Minutes   Serves: 4

Ingredients:

- 400g Brussels Sprouts, halved
- 200g Bacon Lardons
- 1/2 tsp Garlic Granules
- 2 tbsp Parmesan Cheese (optional)
- Salt and Pepper to season

Directions:

1. Slice the Brussels sprouts in half and place them in a bowl.
2. Sprinkle with the garlic granules and salt and pepper to taste. Toss the sprouts about so that they all get covered.
3. Add in the bacon lardons and mix.
4. Transfer to the air fryer basket and cook at 180°C for 15 to 20 minutes.

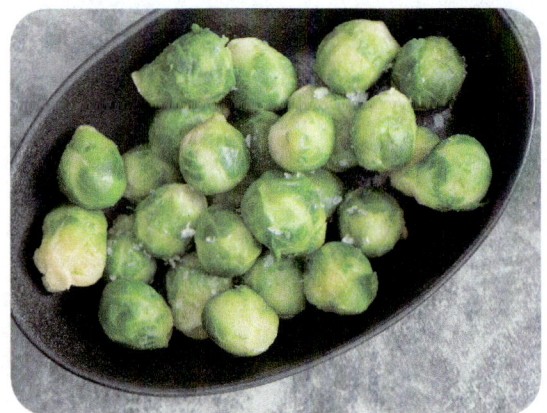

Check on them halfway through and give them a shake. They are ready when they are soft on the inside and browned on the outside.

5. Sprinkle with cheese, either 1 minute before the end of the cooking time or while they are still hot so that the cheese can melt a little bit (optional)

Nutritional Value (Amount per Serving):

Calories: 214; Fat: 15.78; Carb: 13.64; Protein: 9.68

Air Fryer Broccoli

Prep Time: 5 Minutes
Cook Time: 10-15 Minutes   Serves:

Ingredients:

- 1 head Broccoli
- 2 tsp Garlic Powder
- 2 tsp onion powder
- 1-2 tbsp Olive Oil
- Parmesan Cheese (optional)

Directions:

1. Preheat the air fryer to 190°C.
2. Prepare the broccoli by breaking up the florets into evenly sized pieces. Use a sharp knife to slice up any larger florets.
3. In a bowl mix the olive oil and seasoning and stir.
4. Add the sliced broccoli to the bowl and roll it about to roughly coat it.
5. Place the broccoli in the air fryer basket (Depending on the size of the air fryer you might need to cook it in batches)
6. Cook for 10 to 15 minutes, checking on it at 5 minutes to give it a shake. Depending on the size of the broccoli it might cook in more or less time so keep an eye on it. The broccoli is ready when it is tender and starting to brown and crisp up.
7. Sprinkle with parmesan cheese before serving (optional).

Nutritional Value (Amount per Serving):

Calories: 342; Fat: 28.44; Carb: 13.07; Protein: 10.5

Air Fryer Garlic and Herb Potatoes

Prep Time: 5 Minutes
Cook Time: 20 Minutes   Serves:

Ingredients:

- 1kg New Potatoes
- 2-3 Sprigs Rosemary
- Handful Fresh Parsley
- 2 tbsp Garlic Granules/Powder
- 2 tsp Salt
- 2 tbsp Olive Oil

Directions:

1. Chop the potatoes into even-sized chunks, halving the medium ones and quartering the large ones.
2. Finely chop the parsley and the rosemary (leaves only).
3. Place the potatoes in a large bowl, and sprinkle over the chopped herbs, the garlic granules and salt. Drizzle over with olive oil and mix until all potatoes are well coated.
4. Cook in air fryer at 200°C for 20 minutes, shaking after 10 minutes. If you have a smaller air fryer, you may have to cook for longer or in 2 smaller batches.

Nutritional Value (Amount per Serving):

Calories: 1077; Fat: 28.2; Carb: 189.39; Protein: 23.52

Air Fryer Hasselback Potatoes

Prep Time: 5 Minutes
Cook Time: 30-40 Minutes   Serves: 4

Ingredients:

- 4 Medium Potatoes
- Salt and Pepper
- Spray Oil
- Garlic Butter – to make this mix together butter and fresh garlic or garlic powder

Directions:

1. Slice the potatoes 3/4 of the way through. Be sure to use a sharp knife and do not slice all the way through the potato.

2. Use spray oil on the potatoes.
3. Season with salt and pepper.
4. Brush each of the slices on both sides using melted garlic butter.
5. Cook at 180°C for 15 minutes.
6. Remove using tongs. Place on to a chopping board.
7. Completely baste/brush all of the slices again.
8. Cook at 180°C for another 10 minutes.
9. Brush/baste the potatoes again.
10. Cook at 180°C for another 5-10 minutes, depending on the size.

Nutritional Value (Amount per Serving):

Calories: 301; Fat: 1.7; Carb: 65.58; Protein: 7.62

Air Fryer Onions

Prep Time: 2 Minutes
Cook Time: 14-19 Minutes   Serves: 3

Ingredients:

- 1 White Onion
- 1 tbspVegetable Oil
- 1/8 tsp White Sugar

Directions:

1. Chop off both ends of your onion and peel away the skin.
2. Cut the onion in half.
3. Slice each half into semi-circle shapes, around 1/2 cm thick.
4. Lightly dress the onions with your oil. Don't add the sugar yet.
5. Lay the onions in the air fryer basket, or underneath if you're cooking other items at the same time.
6. Cook at 150°C for 6 minutes, stirring halfway through.
7. Add the sugar and mix well to ensure all the onions have a little coating.
8. Cook at 150°C for another 8 minutes, stirring halfway through.
9. If you want grilled caramelised style onions then you can remove them now.
10. If you want very crispy onions then you can continue cooking for another 4-5 minutes, at 150°C, until they are super crispy.

Nutritional Value (Amount per Serving):

Calories: 55; Fat: 4.57; Carb: 3.52; Protein: 0.4

Air Fryer Carrot Fries

Prep Time: 5 Minutes
Cook Time: 15-16 Minutes   Serves: 2

Ingredients:

- 3 Carrots
- 1 tbsp Cornflour
- 1 Garlic Clove
- Salt and Pepper
- 1/2 tbsp Olive Oil

Directions:

1. Top and tail the carrots, then peel if desired.
2. Slice lengthways and then slice lengthways again (or you could use a potato chipper)
3. Roll the carrot fries in the cornflour and season with salt and pepper.
4. Place in the air fryer basket. Try to avoid overlapping as you want to leave lots of room for air distribution for even cooking to occur.
5. Cook at 200°C for 12 minutes initially. Halfway through pour the oil on to the fries and shake well, then continue cooking.
6. If required you can cook for an additional 3-4 minutes.
8. 15-16 minutes is usually sufficient time to cook well, but this depends on the size of the fries - aim for even sizes to ensure even cooking.
9. Once cooked I love to serve alongside a tasty sriracha mayo or even just lightly spread with the homemade garlic butter.

Nutritional Value (Amount per Serving):

Calories: 98; Fat: 3.95; Carb: 15.35; Protein: 1.77

Air Fryer Parsnips Recipe (Honey Glazed)

Prep Time: 5 Minutes
Cook Time: 15-18 Minutes   Serves: 2

Ingredients:

- 250g Parsnips
- Salt Pepper to taste
- 15 ml Honey

Directions:

1. Wash and peel the parsnips.
2. Slice them lengthways into 4 or 6 pieces, depending on the size and length of parsnips.
3. Drizzle over the honey.
4. Add your seasoning.
5. Place the honey glazed parsnips into the air fryer.
6. Cook at 200°C for approximately 18 minutes. Start checking from 15 minutes onwards.

Nutritional Value (Amount per Serving):

Calories: 749; Fat: 0.42; Carb: 199.84; Protein: 2.59

Air Fryer Roasted Tomatoes

Prep Time: 2 Minutes
Cook Time: 20 Minutes   Serves: 4

Ingredients:

- 8 Tomatoes
- 15ml Vegetable Oil
- 4 Cloves Garlic
- 10 Sprigs Thyme
- 1 Sprig Rosemary
- Generous pinch Salt and Pepper

Directions:

1. Wash the tomatoes. Dry thoroughly.
2. Place in a bowl with the vegetable oil and garlic cloves.
3. Mix well until all the tomatoes are coated. 4. Add the herbs, salt and pepper.
5. Cook at 200°C for 20 minutes. Check at the 10-minute mark and shake gently if needed, although you shouldn't need to!

Nutritional Value (Amount per Serving):

Calories: 937; Fat: 102.79; Carb: 12.29; Protein: 2.73

Chapter 3: Poultry

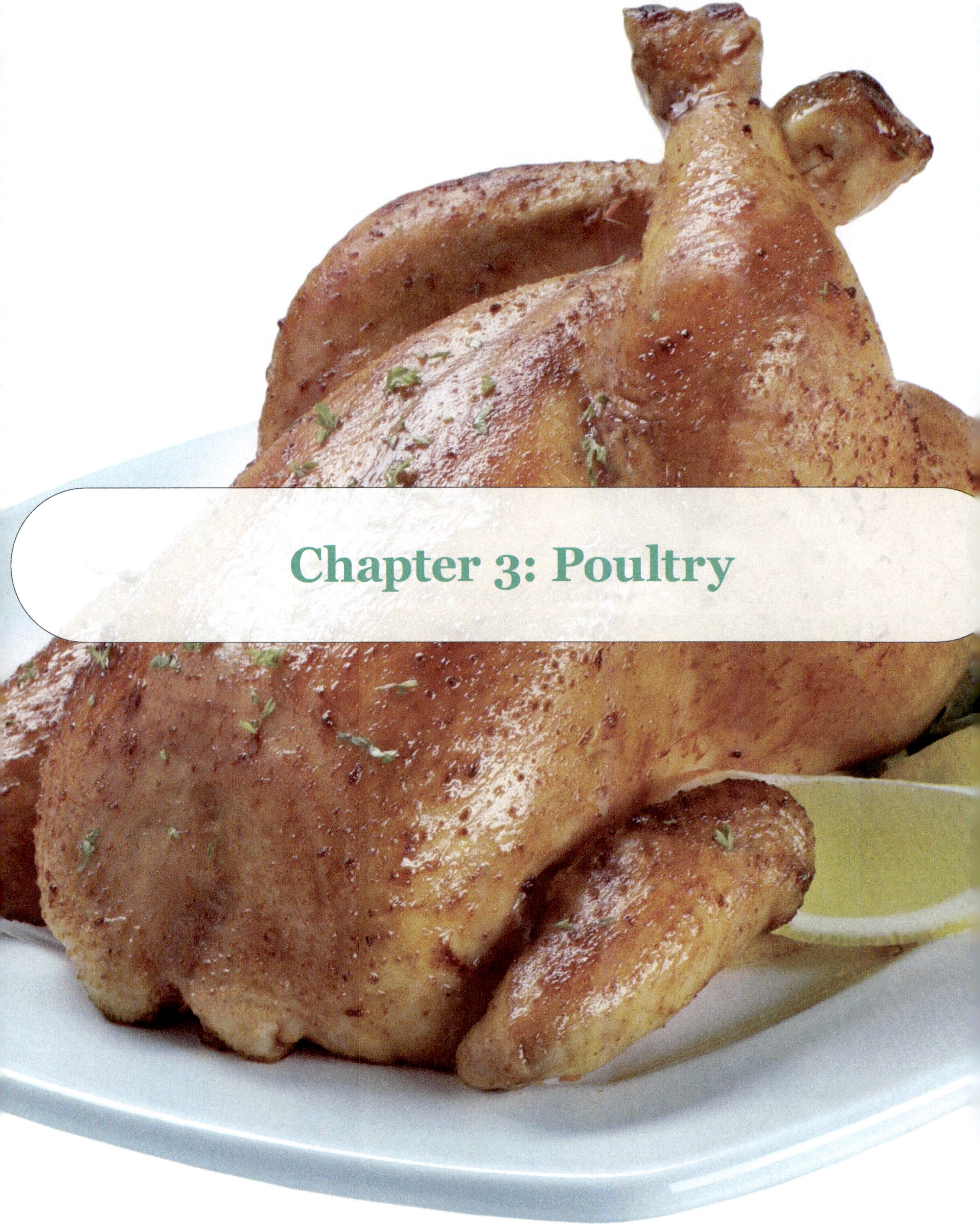

Air Fryer Chicken Thighs

Prep Time: 5 Minutes
Cook Time: 20-25 Minutes   Serves:

Ingredients:

- 1kg Chicken Thighs
- 2 tsp Season All

Directions:

1. Preheat air fryer to 200°C.
2. Pat chicken thighs dry with some kitchen paper before seasoning.
3. Put seasoned chicken thighs in the hot air fryer. Depending on the size of your air fryer you may need to do this in batches, or, if you can, use a trivet or shelf.
4. Cook for 10 minutes before turning the thighs over. Cook for a further 10 minutes. They should be crispy and cooked through - if they are not, return them to the air fryer for a further 5 minutes, or until they are cooked. The internal temperature should be 75°C.
5. Serve with your favourite side dish!

Nutritional Value (Amount per Serving):

Calories: 3358; Fat: 224.5; Carb: 145.61; Protein: 186.86

Air Fryer Piri Piri Chicken Legs

Prep Time: 5 Minutes
Cook Time: 22 Minutes   Serves: 4

Ingredients:

- 4 Chicken Legs
- 2 tsp Piri Piri Spice Mix
- 120g Piri Piri Marinade Sauce (approx)

Directions:

1. Add the spice mix and sauce to the raw chicken legs. Leave them to marinate for around 30 minutes.
2. Transfer to the air fryer basket and cook at 190°C for 22 minutes.

3. Turn the chicken legs at the halfway mark.
4. The chicken legs are ready when the juices run clear and the internal temperature is 75°C, use a meat thermometer if necessary.

Nutritional Value (Amount per Serving):

Calories: 345; Fat: 11.19; Carb: 4.87; Protein: 52.55

Air Fryer Chicken Breasts

Prep Time: 10 Minutes
Cook Time: 20 Minutes   Serves: 1

Ingredients:

- 1 Chicken Breast (increase accordingly)
- 1/2 tbsp Olive Oil
- 1/2 tsp Salt
- 1/2 tsp Pepper
- 1/2 tsp Garlic Powder (or seasoning of your choice)

Directions:

1. Preheat the air fryer to 180°C.
2. Brush or spray each chicken breast with the olive oil.
3. Season one side (the smooth side) of each chicken breast.
4. Place each chicken breast (smooth side down) in the air fryer basket. Season the other side.
5. Set the timer for 10 minutes.
6. After 10 minutes turn the chicken breasts over and cook for a further 10 minutes to allow them to cook on both sides.
7. Check the chicken is cooked all the way through - use a meat thermometer if necessary.
8. Leave the chicken to rest for 5 minutes before serving or slicing.

Nutritional Value (Amount per Serving):

Calories: 143; Fat: 8.42; Carb: 0.82; Protein: 15.29

Air Fryer Chicken Wings

Prep Time: 5 Minutes
Cook Time: 20-25 Minutes   Serves: 4

Ingredients:

- 1kg Chicken Wings
- 1 tbsp Olive Oil
- ½ tsp Garlic Powder
- ½ tsp Onion Powder
- ½ tsp Paprika
- ½ tsp Salt
- ½ tsp Black Pepper

Directions:

1. Preheat the air fryer to 180°C.
2. Prepare the chicken wings by patting them dry with some kitchen roll. (The drier the chicken wings are, the crispier they will come out.)
3. Add the wings to a large bowl and cover with the olive oil, tossing them so that they are all covered as much as possible.
4. Add all the seasonings, coating all the wings.
5. Put the chicken wings in the air fryer. Depending on how many wings you are cooking, and the size of your air fryer, you might need to do them in batches. You can also use a rack in your air fryer to fit more in. The key thing is to make sure the wings are not touching each other so that they have room to crisp up.
6. Cook for 20 minutes, turning and shaking 2 or 3 times to ensure they cook evenly.
7. Increase the temperature to 200°C and cook for a further 5 minutes or until the skin is crispy.
8. Serve with BBQ sauce, Hot Pepper Sauce, Buffalo Sauce, etc

Nutritional Value (Amount per Serving):

Calories: 561; Fat: 35.11; Carb: 9.28; Protein: 49.35

Air Fryer Hunters Chicken

Prep Time: 5 Minutes
Cook Time: 25 Minutes   Serves: 2

Ingredients:

- 2 Chicken Breasts (1 per person)
- 4 Rashers of Bacon (2 per chicken piece)
- 6 tbsp BBQ Sauce
- 50g grated Cheese (cheddar, mozzarella, gouda or parmesan)

Directions:

1. Place the chicken breasts in the air fryer basket at 190°C and set the timer for 10 minutes. Turn the chicken at the 5-minute mark.
2. After 10 minutes of cooking time, using tongs or a fork, remove the chicken breasts and wrap each one in two rashers of bacon (use a cocktail stick to keep these in place.
3. Return the bacon-wrapped chicken to the air fryer basket and cook for a further 10 minutes, again turning halfway.
4. At the end of the cooking time, open the air fryer basket and brush the BBQ sauce equally over each chicken breast.
5. Sprinkle the grated cheese over the top of the BBQ sauce.
6. Air fry for a further 2 to 3 minutes or until the cheese has melted and the BBQ sauce is hot.
7. Remove from the air fryer and remove the cocktail sticks.
8. Check the chicken is cooked all the way through, either by cutting into one or using a meat thermometer.
9. Serve with your favourite side dish.

Nutritional Value (Amount per Serving):

Calories: 1803; Fat: 118.5; Carb: 3.96; Protein: 169.98

Air Fryer BBQ Chicken Breast

Prep Time: 3 Minutes
Cook Time: 20 Minutes   Serves: 2

Ingredients:

- 2 Chicken Breasts (1 per person)
- Spray Oil
- Salt and Pepper
- Smoked Paprika
- Garlic Salt or Garlic Powder
- 80ml BBQ Sauce

Directions:

1. Spray the chicken breasts with spray oil.
2. Mix together the smoked paprika, garlic salt, salt and pepper then sprinkle onto the chicken.
3. Turn the chicken over and repeat this step again.
4. Lay the chicken in the air fryer basket.
5. Cook at 180°C for 10 minutes.
6. Turn over the chicken breast.
7. Cook at 180°C for another 8 minutes.
8. Pour over the barbecue sauce (I like to use a silicone pastry brush to ensure even coverage, but you can just use a spoon or whatever you have to hand).
9. Cook at 180°C for another 2 minutes.
10. Check the internal temperature of the chicken breast (in the thickest part) is a minimum of 74°C and then remove.
11. Rest the chicken for 5 minutes before you slice and serve. Or just serve up as a whole chicken breast alongside the rest of your dinner.

Nutritional Value (Amount per Serving):

Calories: 477; Fat: 15.95; Carb: 80.18; Protein: 20.21

Air Fryer Cajun Chicken

Prep Time: 5 Minutes
Cook Time: 20 Minutes   Serves: 4

Ingredients:

- 640g Chicken Mini Fillets
- Cajun Seasoning

Directions:

1. Add chicken to a bowl.
2. Add the cajun seasoning and rub all over the chicken fillets.
3. Lightly oil the air fryer basket (I use spray rapeseed oil)
4. Add your chicken mini fillets to the air fryer.
5. Cook on 200°C for 20 minutes, turning 10 minutes in.
6. If you overload the air fryer basket a little, like me, then you'll want to give these a shake a couple of times during the 20 minutes.
7. Check the temperature before serving. Chicken should be at least 74°C internally before serving.

Nutritional Value (Amount per Serving):

Calories: 462; Fat: 18.08; Carb: 51.76; Protein: 22.3

Air Fryer Chicken Nachos

Prep Time: 5 Minutes
Cook Time: 5 Minutes   Serves: 1

Ingredients:

- 65g Tortilla Chips
- 100g Chopped Cooked Chicken (I used Air Fryer Cajun Chicken recipe on page 45)
- 20g Sour Cream • 20g Guacamole
- 20g Salsa   • 20g Cheese Sauce
- 30g Grated Cheese

Directions:

1. Line the air fryer basket with baking paper. Do not use aluminium foil as this will stick to the nachos and can also be unsuitable for air frying

2. Spread out the tortilla chips.
3. Share the sour cream, guacamole, salsa, cheese sauce and chopped chicken across the tortilla chips.
4. Add the grated cheese over the top covering as much of the dish as possible.
5. Air fry at 200°C for 5 minutes.

Nutritional Value (Amount per Serving):

Calories: 376; Fat: 15.33; Carb: 48.28; Protein: 12.56

Air Fryer Chicken Parmesan

Prep Time: 10 Minutes
Cook Time: 16-18 Minutes   Serves: 4

Ingredients:

- 2 Large Boneless Chicken Breasts
- Salt
- Freshly Ground Black Pepper
- 40g Plain Flour   • 2 Large Eggs
- 100g Panko Breadcrumbs
- 25g Freshly Grated Parmesan Cheese
- 1 tsp Dried Oregano
- 1/2 tsp Garlic Powder
- 1/2 tsp Chilli Flakes   • 240g Marinara/Tomato Sauce
- 100g Grated Mozzarella • Freshly Chopped Parsley, for garnish

Directions:

1. Carefully butterfly chicken by cutting in half widthwise to create 4 thin pieces of chicken. Season on both sides with salt and pepper.
2. Prepare dredging station: Place flour in a shallow bowl and season with a large pinch of salt and pepper. Place eggs in a second bowl and beat. In a third bowl, combine breadcrumbs, Parmesan cheese, oregano, garlic powder, and chilli flakes.
3. Working with one piece of a chicken at a time, coat in flour, then dip in egg, and finally press into Panko mixture making sure both sides are coated well.
4. Working in batches as necessary, place chicken in basket of air fryer and cook at 200°C for 5 minutes on each side. Top chicken with sauce and mozzarella and cook at 200°C for 3 minutes more or until cheese is melty and golden.
5. Garnish with parsley to serve.

Nutritional Value (Amount per Serving):

Calories: 633; Fat: 23.16; Carb: 37.03; Protein: 63.72

Chapter 4: Meats

Air Fryer Sausages

Prep Time: 3 Minutes
Cook Time: 10 Minutes   Serves: 8

Ingredients:

- 8 Sausages

Directions:

1. Preheat the air fryer to 180°C.
2. Pierce each sausage with a knife or fork.
3. Lay sausages in the air fryer basket.
4. Cook for 10 minutes, checking on them and turning them over after 5 minutes.

Nutritional Value (Amount per Serving):

Calories: 73; Fat: 5.15; Carb: 2.79; Protein: 5.25

Air Fryer Meatballs

Prep Time: 10 Minutes
Cook Time: 7-15 Minutes   Serves:

Ingredients:

- 500g Lean Beef Mince
- 1 Clove Garlic, crushed
- 1 tsp Dried Mixed Herbs
- 1 Egg
- 1tbsp Breadcrumbs, (optional)

Directions:

1. Mix all ingredients together until well combined.
2. Using your hands, form small round balls (this recipe makes about 16, depending on size of meatballs)
3. Place meatballs in air fryer and cook at 180°C for 7 minutes. Check halfway through and turn over if necessary.
4. If you want to add a sauce, once the meatballs are cooked transfer them to an ovenproof dish/pan that will fit in the air fryer. Pour your choice of tomato sauce on top and place container in air fryer tray. Cook at 180°C for about 6-8 minutes, or until the sauce is warmed through.
5. Serve with spaghetti and melted cheese.

Nutritional Value (Amount per Serving):

Calories: 799; Fat: 38.2; Carb: 2.02; Protein: 111.76

Air Fryer Pork Chops

Prep Time: 5 Minutes
Cook Time: 12 Minutes   Serves: 1

Ingredients:

- 1 Pork Chop
- 1/2 tbsp Olive Oil
- 1/2 tbsp Seasoning

Directions:

1. Preheat the air fryer to 200°C.
2. Brush oil on each side of the pork chop.
3. Add seasoning and rub it in evenly all over.
4. Place pork chop in the preheated air fryer and set the timer for 12 minutes. Turn the pork chop over at around the 6-minute mark.
5. Check the pork chop is cooked all the way through - it should be golden brown on the outside and juices should run clear.

Nutritional Value (Amount per Serving):

Calories: 402; Fat: 24.16; Carb: 2.49; Protein: 40.4

Crispy Air Fryer Bacon

Prep Time: 5 Minutes
Cook Time: 10 Minutes   Serves: 8

Ingredients:

- 340 g Thick-Cut Bacon

Directions:

1. Lay bacon inside air fryer basket in a single layer.
2. Set air fryer to 200°C and cook until crispy, about 10 minutes. (You can check halfway through and rearrange slices with tongs.)

Nutritional Value (Amount per Serving):

Calories: 132; Fat: 12.55; Carb: 2.69; Protein: 4.54

Air Fryer Frozen Sausages

Prep Time: 5 Minutes
Cook Time: 20-25 Minutes   Serves: 4

Ingredients:

- 4 Frozen Sausages (Chicken, Beef or Pork)

Directions:

1. Put the frozen sausages in the air fryer basket.
2. Air fry at a temperature of 160°C for 4 minutes.
3. Bring air fryer basket out and use a spatula to separate the sausages
4. Put the basket back in the air fryer and cook sausages at 160°C for 15- 20 minutes (flipping them with tongs halfway into cooking) or until cooked.
5. Bring out the sausages and serve.

Nutritional Value (Amount per Serving):

Calories: 1166; Fat: 82.37; Carb: 44.63; Protein: 84.05

Thai Green Fish Curry

Prep Time: 10 Minutes
Cook Time: 28-30 Minutes   Serves: 4

Ingredients:

- 400g Skinless White Fish, such as cod, monkfish or haddock
ForMarinade
- 1 tbsp Vegetable Oil
- 3 tbsp Thai Green Curry Paste
- 2 tsp Korma Paste
For the Sauce
- 1 Large Onion (300g), peeled and chopped
- 1 tbsp Vegetable Oil
- 2 Garlic Cloves, peeled and grated
- 3 Fresh or Dried Kaffir Lime Leaves (optional)
- 400g tin Coconut Milk
- 2 tsp Freshly Grated Ginger
- 1 tsp Turmeric

- 10g Fresh Basil, roughly chopped
- 10g Fresh Coriander
- 1 Red Pepper, deseeded and thinly sliced
- 50g Sugar Snaps, halved lengthways

Directions:

1. Cut the fish into bite sized chunks then mix the marinade ingredients together in a bowl, add the fish and toss gently until the fish is coated.
2. Next, place the onion in a deep roasting dish that fits the air fryer, drizzle with oil and set the air fryer temperature to 180°C and cook for 5 minutes until the onion has softened.
3. Add the garlic, ginger, turmeric, lime leaves and a drizzle of oil then cook for another 3 minutes. Remove the dish from the air fryer and put the onion mixture into a large jug with the coconut milk, basil and coriander. Blitz with a hand blender until smooth.
4. Place the pepper and sugar snaps in the bottom of the dish, followed by a layer of fish, then pour over the sauce and gently stir to combine. Set the air fryer temperature to 180°C and cook for 20 minutes or until the sauce is piping hot and the fish is cooked.

Nutritional Value (Amount per Serving):

Calories: 1003; Fat: 68.05; Carb: 37.7; Protein: 63.91

Lamb Rump With Mint and Rosemary

Prep Time: 10 Minutes
Cook Time: 25 Minutes   Serves: 4

Ingredients:

- 4 x 150g Lamb Rump
- 1 tbsp Olive Oil

For the Mint and Rosemary Butter
- 45g Butter, softened
- 2 Sprigs Rosemary, leaves finely chopped
- 1 Small Bunch Mint, leaves finely chopped

For the Crushed Potatoes
- 1kg New Potatoes, washed
- 20g Butter
- Salt and Black Pepper

Directions:

1. Place the lamb on a plate, season with salt and black pepper, drizzle with 2

tsp oil and leave to one side to bring the meat to room temperature.

2. Meanwhile, to make butter; mix the butter, rosemary and half of the chopped mint, then shape into a sausage shape. Wrap in cling film and pop in the fridge to firm up.

3. Bring a pan of water to the boil then add the new potatoes, bring to the boil and simmer for 15-20 minutes until tender. Drain the potatoes in a colander then return to the pan, add 20g of butter and the remaining mint and roughly smash with a potato masher. Cover and keep warm.

4. Meanwhile insert the 10-in-1 wire rack into the air fryer with the grill plate, flat side up, on top of the wire rack. Set the temperature to 180°C and preheat the grill plate for 3 minutes. Carefully add the lamb to the grill and cook for 4 minutes, then turn and cook for another 4 minutes.

5. Carefully remove the rack and grill plate out of the air fryer and put onto a heatproof surface to cool. (Wear oven gloves to remove the wire rack and grill plate from the air fryer as they will be very hot). Transfer the lamb onto a plate, cut the butter into 4 discs and place one on each lamb steak. Cover with foil and allow the lamb to rest and melt the butter.

6. Serve the lamb and herb butter with the crushed potatoes on the side.

Nutritional Value (Amount per Serving):

Calories: 479; Fat: 19.55; Carb: 70.21; Protein: 8.64

Thai Style Grilled Mackerel

Prep Time: 5 Minutes
Cook Time: 20 Minutes   Serves: 4

Ingredients:

- 4 Mackerel Fillets 90g each, skin on
For the Marinade
- 90g Green Thai Paste
- 1 tsp Ground Turmeric
- 1 tsp Garlic Paste
- 1 tbsp Light Soy Sauce
For the Rice
- 200g Basmati Rice
- 400ml Vegetable Stock
- 150g Sugar Snaps, cut into thirds
- 1 Red Pepper, thinly sliced
- 1 Lime, zest grated then cut into wedges
- 1 Small Bunch Coriander, roughly chopped

Directions:

1. Mix the marinade ingredients together in a bowl then put the fish, skin side down, on a shallow tray. Pour the marinade over the fish, cover and refrigerate for 30 minutes for the flavours to develop.
2. Bring a pan of water to the boil, add the rice then cover and simmer for 10 minutes. Add the sugar snaps and red pepper to the rice and quickly place the lid back on the pan. Take the pan off the heat and allow the contents to cook in their own steam for a further 10 minutes.
3. When the rice has about 10 minutes left to cook, insert the 10-in-1 wire rack into the air fryer with the grill plate, flat side up, on top of the wire rack. Set the temperature to 180°C and preheat the grill plate for 3 minutes.
4. Place the fish onto the grill plate, flesh side down, cook for 7 minutes, then carefully turn the fish and brush the flesh with any reserved marinade. Cook for further 5 minutes, or until the fish is cooked to your liking.
5. Carefully remove the rack and grill plate from the air fryer and put onto a heatproof surface to cool (wear oven gloves to remove the wire rack and grill plate from the air fryer as they will be very hot).
6. Season the rice, stir through lime zest and serve on plates, with a piece of mackerel on top, then garnish with chopped coriander.

Nutritional Value (Amount per Serving):

Calories: 1454; Fat: 124.4; Carb: 58.43; Protein: 35.65

Teriyaki and Sesame Salmon Skewers

Prep Time: 10 Minutes
Cook Time: 30 Minutes   Serves: 4

Ingredients:

- 3 tbsp Teriyaki Sauce
- 2 tbsp Honey
- 2 tbsp Light Soy Sauce
- 1 Clove Garlic, grated or crushed
- 500g Skinless Salmon
- 300g Tender Stem Broccoli
- 200g Sugar Snaps
- 240g Jasmine Rice
- 1 Lime
- Vegetable oil spray in a bottle
- 1½ tsp Sesame Seeds
- 2 tsp Sesame Oil

Directions:

1. Pour the teriyaki sauce, honey, soy sauce and garlic into a bowl, stir to combine. Cut the salmon fillets into 2cm wide pieces, pop into the marinade and mix well to coat. Cover and set aside in the fridge to marinate for an hour.
2. Meanwhile cut the tender stem broccoli lengthways (if it is thick) then cut into thirds and cut the sugar snaps in half.
3. Bring a pan of water to the boil, add the rice then cook for 15 minutes until tender, drain and return the rice to the pan then cover with a lid to keep warm. Zest the lime and cut into wedges.
4. When ready to cook, evenly thread the salmon onto 4 kebab skewers, spray lightly with oil and sprinkle over the sesame seeds. Reserve any remaining marinade and transfer to a small pan.
5. Rest the skewers in the grooves on the edges of the multi-function rack and insert into the air fryer with the non-stick oil tray below. Set the air fryer temperature to 180C and cook the skewers for 15 minutes until the salmon is heated through and is slightly charred; Carefully remove from the oven using the heat proof finger mitts supplied. You will need to cook the kebabs in two batches.
6. Meanwhile, heat the sesame oil in a wok or frying pan and stir fry the broccoli and sugar snaps for 4-5 minutes until charred.
7. Gently heat the remaining marinade and stir the lime zest through the rice.
8. Serve the rice on warm plates topped with the salmon kebabs with the stir fry vegetables on the side. Finally, drizzle over the remaining marinade.

Nutritional Value (Amount per Serving):

Calories: 721; Fat: 25.01; Carb: 83.87; Protein: 42.37

Chapter 5: Casseroles, Frittatas, and Quiches

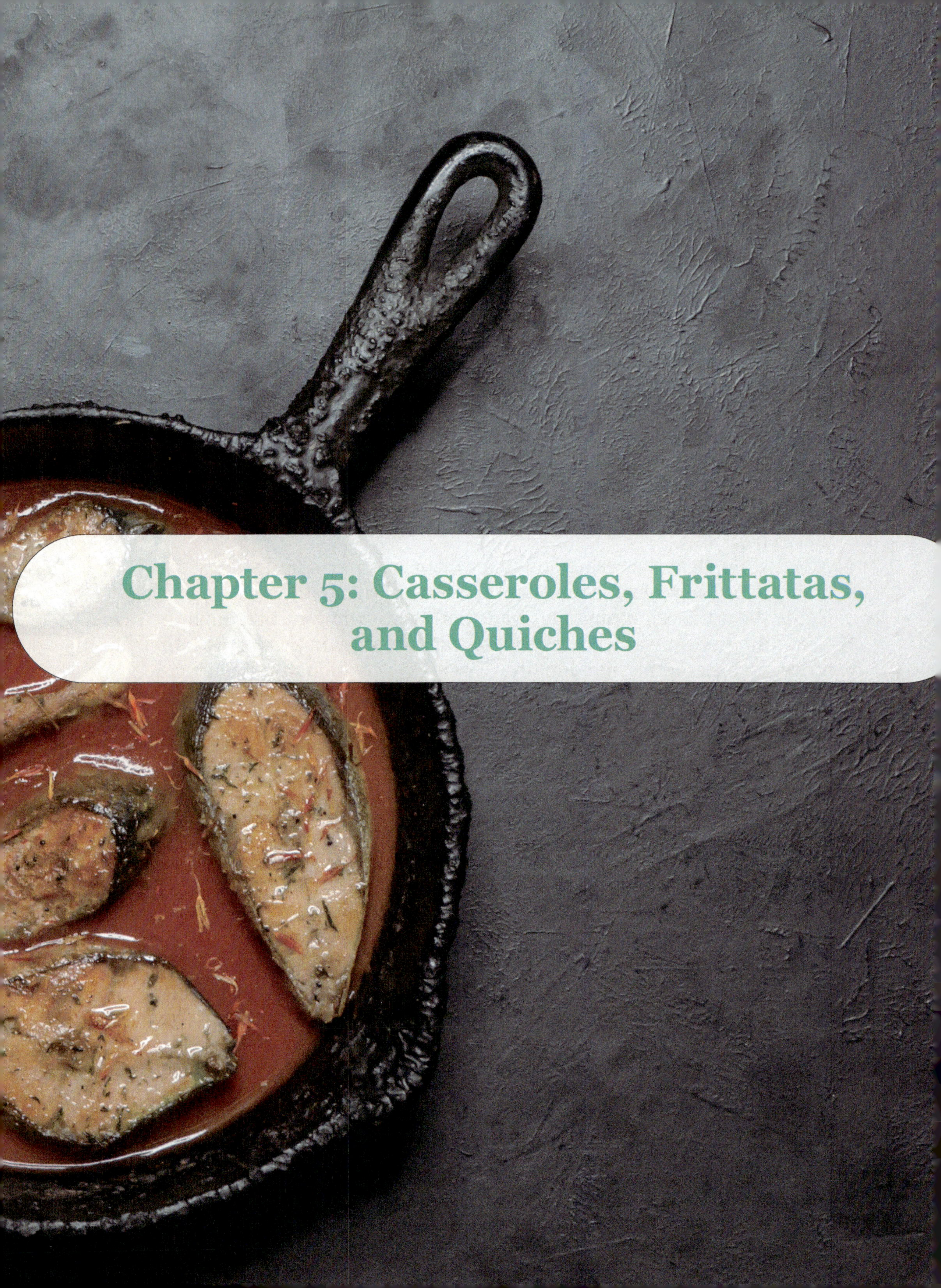

Air Fryer Frozen Hash Browns

Prep Time: 1 Minute
Cook Time: 15-17 Minutes   Serves: 8

Ingredients:

- 8 Frozen Hash Browns

Directions:

1. Add individually frozen hash browns to the air fryer basket.
2. Air fry at 180°C for 15 minutes, and flip over halfway through. The hash browns should be crispy and golden brown on each side. If not, return to the air fryer for a further minute or two.

Nutritional Value (Amount per Serving):

Calories: 62; Fat: 3.29; Carb: 8.08; Protein: 0.75

Air Fryer Tortilla Pizza

Prep Time: 1 Minute
Cook Time: 5 Minutes   Serves: 1

Ingredients:

- 1 Tortilla
- 30 ml Pizza Sauce
- Pepperoni or other toppings
- 30 g Grated Mozzarella Cheese
- Herbs (fresh or dried)

Directions:

1. Place the tortilla on a chopping board.
2. Spread pizza sauce over the tortilla.
   You can easily make your own pizza sauce with a little passata and tomato puree mixed together with a little garlic powder, basil and oregano.
3. Add the meat or other pizza toppings.
4. Add the cheese last. As the air fryer has a lot of airflow, place the pepperoni under the mozzarella, otherwise it may be blown off the pizza.
5. Line the air fryer with baking paper, to prevent sticking..
6. There is no need to preheat the air fryer for this recipe.

7. Cook at 200°C for 5 minutes.
8. Top with a sprinkling of herbs.
9. Slice, serve and enjoy! It goes GREAT with air fryer garlic bread too.

Nutritional Value (Amount per Serving):

Calories: 956; Fat: 32.49; Carb: 119.76; Protein: 45.28

Air Fryer Grilled Ham and Cheese

Prep Time: 2 Minutes
Cook Time: 10 Minutes   Serves: 1

Ingredients:

- 2 Slices of Crusty Bread
- 40g Sliced or Grated Cheddar Cheese
- 2 Slices Cooked Ham of Choice
- 10g Margarine or Mayonnaise (your choice)

Directions:

1. Preheat the air fryer basket to 180°C for 1-2 minutes.
2. Spread the outside of the bread with butter or mayonnaise
3. Make up the sandwich with cheese and ham.
4. Cook for 10 minutes at 180°C and turn 5 minutes in.
5. Serve the grilled ham and cheese with your choice of crisps or even a nice side salad to make it a little more balanced.

Nutritional Value (Amount per Serving):

Calories: 295; Fat: 14.47; Carb: 24.57; Protein: 16.7

Air Fryer Chimichanga

Prep Time: 15 Minutes
Cook Time: 15-20 Minutes   Serves: 8

Ingredients:

- 1 tbsp Extra-Virgin Olive Oil
- 1 Small Yellow Onion, chopped
- 2 Cloves Garlic, crushed
- 1 tsp Chilli Powder
- 1 tsp Ground Cumin
- 1/2 tsp Garlic Powder

- 195g Salsa
- 560g Shredded Cooked Chicken
- Salt
- Freshly Ground Black Pepper
- 120g Sour Cream, plus more for serving
- Cooking Spray
- 1 x 400g can Refried Beans
- 8 Large Flour Tortillas
- 100g Grated Cheddar Cheese
- 100g Grated Pepper Jack Cheese
- Guacamole, for serving

Directions:

1. Heat the oil in a medium pan over medium heat. Add onions and cook until soft, approx. 5 minutes. Add garlic, chilli powder, cumin, and garlic powder. Cook until fragrant, about 1 minute. Add salsa and bring to a simmer, then add shredded chicken and toss to coat. Season with salt and pepper. Remove from heat.
2. Spread about 65g of refried beans in centre of tortilla, then sprinkle with both cheeses. Top with about 70g of chicken mixture and some sour cream. Roll into a burrito by folding the top and bottom of tortilla into the centre, then fold the right side all the way over the filling, tucking and rolling tightly. Set aside on a plate, seam side down, and repeat with remaining tortillas and filling.
3. Working in batches as necessary, place burritos into basket of air fryer, seam side down, and spray with a little cooking spray. Cook at 200°C for 5 minutes, then flip, spray with more cooking spray, and cook another 5 minutes.
4. Drizzle with more sour cream and serve with guacamole.

Nutritional Value (Amount per Serving):

Calories: 783; Fat: 52.21; Carb: 28.95; Protein: 47.66

Pesto and Mozzarella Pinwheels

Prep Time: 10 Minutes
Cook Time: 20 Minutes   Serves: 12

Ingredients:

- 375g Sheet of Ready Rolled Puff Pastry
- 75g Green Pesto
- 120g Roasted Pepper, from a jar, finely chopped
- 20g Grated Parmesan Cheese
- 50g Hard Mozzarella, grated
- 1 Egg, beaten

Directions:

1. Unroll the pastry, then spread the pesto across, leaving approximately a

1cm edge around the pastry.

2. Place the peppers evenly across the pesto, then top with a sprinkling of parmesan and mozzarella cheeses.
3. Brush the edges of the pastry with beaten egg, roll up from the side, like a Swiss roll.
4. Press firmly to seal, then slice into 12 equal sized pieces and lay flat on two air flow racks lined with parchment paper.
5. Set the air fryer temperature to 190°C and preheat for 3 minutes.
6. Brush the pinwheels with beaten egg and place the racks on the top and middle shelves for 20 minutes, or until golden and well risen. Rotate the racks halfway through cooking.

Nutritional Value (Amount per Serving):

Calories: 76; Fat: 3.06; Carb: 7.84; Protein: 4.35

Roast Chicken and Pesto Traybake

Prep Time: 10 Minutes
Cook Time: 30 Minutes   Serves: 4

Ingredients:

- 2 tbsp Olive Oil
- 4 Medium Sized Chicken Breasts
- 50g Fresh Green Pesto
- 35g Fresh White Breadcrumbs
- 20g Parmesan Cheese
- Olive Oil Spray
- 600g Baby New Potatoes, parboiled
- 220g Cherry Tomatoes on the Vine, cut into little bunches
- Small Bunch Fresh Basil (optional)
- Black Pepper

Directions:

1. Drizzle some oil in the base of a 24cm square roasting tin. Place the chicken breasts into the tray and spread the pesto over the top. Mix the breadcrumbs and parmesan in a small bowl with a teaspoon of olive oil, then cover each chicken breast with a sprinkling of breadcrumbs. Spray each chicken breast lightly with olive oil.
2. Slice the potatoes and arrange evenly over a lightly oiled air flow rack. Spray the potatoes with oil and season with black pepper.
3. Place the roasting tin on the middle shelf of the air fryer, with the potatoes below. Set the temperature to 180°C for 30 minutes.

4. When the chicken has 10 minutes remaining, add the bunches of tomatoes to the roasting tin, sitting them in between the chicken breasts. Move the potatoes to the top shelf to crispen for the last 10 minutes.
5. When the chicken is piping hot, sprinkle some fresh basil leaves over the chicken and serve with the potatoes alongside.

Nutritional Value (Amount per Serving):

Calories: 466; Fat: 18.88; Carb: 49.02; Protein: 27.38

Cheese and Spring Onion Quesadilla

Prep Time: 5 Minutes
Cook Time: 10-12 Minutes   Serves: 4

Ingredients:

- 200g Cheddar Cheese, grated
- 3 tbsp Mayonnaise
- 4 Spring Onions, finely chopped
- 4 x 20cm Soft Tortilla Wraps
- 1 Egg, beaten
- 1 tbsp Olive Oil
- Salt and Black Pepper
- 4 portions Mixed Salad

Directions:

1. Place the grated cheese, mayonnaise and spring onions in a bowl, season with salt and black pepper and mix well to combine.
2. Lay the wraps on a flat surface, brush the edges with egg, then divide the cheese mixture evenly between the wraps. Fold the wraps over like a pasty and press the edges down firmly to seal.
3. Brush the wraps lightly with oil. Set the air fryer temperature to 200°C and place the quesadillas onto the wire toasting rack, making sure that they are evenly spaced. Toast for 10-12 minutes, until the quesadillas are crisp and golden.
4. Cut each quesadilla in half and serve warm with a portion of salad.

Nutritional Value (Amount per Serving):

Calories: 425; Fat: 21.86; Carb: 32.3; Protein: 24

Easy Sage and Onion Stuffing Balls

Prep Time: 3 Minutes
Cook Time: 15 Minutes   Serves: 9

Ingredients:

- 100g Sausage Meat
- ½ Small Onion (peeled and diced)
- ½ tsp Garlic Puree
- 1tsp Sage
- 3tbsp Breadcrumbs
- Salt and Pepper

Directions:

1. Place the ingredients into a mixing bowl and mix well.
2. Form into medium sized balls and place them in the air fryer
3. Cook at 180°C for 15 minutes and then serve.

Nutritional Value (Amount per Serving):

Calories: 73; Fat: 2.55; Carb: 9.46; Protein: 3.52

Chapter 6: Appetizers and Snacks

Air Fryer Chicken Drumsticks

Prep Time: 5 Minutes
Cook Time: 22-25 Minutes   Serves: 8

Ingredients:

- 8-12 Chicken Drumsticks
- Seasoning
- Oil (optional)

Directions:

1. Preheat the air fryer to 200°C for 5 minutes.
2. Brush the drumsticks with some oil.
3. Season the chicken drumsticks with your favourite spices (or you can just use salt if you prefer).
4. Add the drumsticks to the air fryer basket. You might need to use a trivet to fit them all in, or if you have a smaller air fryer, cook them in batches.
5. Cook for 22-25 minutes, turning halfway through.
6. Check the drumsticks are cooked all the way through - they should reach 75°C internally, use a meat thermometer if possible.

Nutritional Value (Amount per Serving):

Calories: 267; Fat: 15.51; Carb: 0.25; Protein: 29.39

Air Fryer Frozen Meatballs

Prep Time: 1 Minutes
Cook Time: 12 Minutes   Serves: 2

Ingredients:

- Cooking Spray
- Frozen Meatballs

Directions:

1. Add a light coating of cooking spray to your air fryer basket.
2. Spread a single layer of frozen meatballs in the fry basket. Be sure not to overcrowd the basket, as this will prevent the meatballs from cooking evenly. If necessary, cook them in batches.
3. Set the air fryer temperature to 200°C and the timer to 6 minutes and let it cook.

4. After 6 minutes, remove the fry basket and give it a good shake to ensure all the meatballs are cooked evenly.
5. Replace the basket and cook for another 6 minutes.
6. Serve with your favorite dipping sauce and enjoy!

Nutritional Value (Amount per Serving):

Calories: 449; Fat: 20.43; Carb: 18.67; Protein: 47.73

Air Fryer Frozen Burgers

Prep Time: 5 Minutes
Cook Time: 20 Minutes   Serves: 2

Ingredients:

- Cooking Spray
- 1-2 Frozen Burger Patties
- Cheese (optional)
- Lettuce, Onions, Pickles, Etc. (Optional)

Directions:

1. Spray the bottom of the air fryer basket with some cooking spray or olive oil.
2. Add 1-2 frozen burger patties to the fry basket. Do not let them overlap each other. Just a little space between them is fine, the burgers will shrink while cooking.
3. Set the temperature to 200°C and the air fryer timer to 13 minutes and let the burgers cook.
4. After 6 minutes, remove the basket and flip the burgers over.
5. Replace the basket and let the burgers cook for the remaining 7 minutes.
6. After cooking for 13 minutes, open the air fryer basket and top your burger with a slice of cheese, replace the fry basket and let it sit for 1 minute. (Optional)
7. Remove the burgers from the air fryer and add your lettuce, onions, pickles, etc (Optional). Enjoy!

Nutritional Value (Amount per Serving):

Calories: 131; Fat: 9.02; Carb: 6.12; Protein: 6.45

Air Fryer Frozen Broccoli

Prep Time: 3 Minutes
Cook Time: 8-10 Minutes   Serves: 2

Ingredients:

- Frozen Broccoli
- Salt and Pepper
- Garlic Powder (Optional)
- Olive Oil Spray (Optional)

Directions:

1. Preheat your air fryer to 360 degrees Fahrenheit for 2 minutes.
2. Place the frozen broccoli in the air fryer, do not allow it to thaw beforehand, do not stack the florets, if your fry basket is large enough, a single layer is perfect.
3. Cook the frozen broccoli at 180°C for 4 minutes. This initial cooking phase is mainly to defrost the broccoli.
4. After 4 minutes, remove the fryer basket and empty the water from the bottom of the fryer.
5. Add salt, black pepper, garlic powder (optional), and a few sprays of olive oil to the broccoli.
6. Replace the air fryer basket and cook for another 4 minutes at the same temperature.
7. Remove the air fryer basket again and add a sprinkle of parmesan cheese to top it off. Enjoy!

Nutritional Value (Amount per Serving):

Calories: 206; Fat: 15.06; Carb: 15.49; Protein: 7.53

Air Fryer Cheese Chips

Prep Time: 3 Minutes
Cook Time: 16 Minutes   Serves: 2

Ingredients:

- 400g Frozen Chips of your choice
- 30g Finely Grated Cheddar Cheese (extra mature works great)
- 10g Parmesan or Pecorino Cheese
- 1/8 tsp Salt

Directions:

1. Preheat the air fryer to 180°C.
2. Add frozen chips to the air fryer basket.
3. Cook for 8 minutes.
4. Shake, turn the air fryer up to 200°C.
5. Cook for a further 6 minutes.
6. Shake the chips well.
7. Top with the grated cheddar and parmesan or pecorino.
8. Cook for a further 2 minutes.
9. Sprinkle on salt, to taste, and serve.

Nutritional Value (Amount per Serving):

Calories: 299; Fat: 8.78; Carb: 46.81; Protein: 10.01

Air Fryer Grilled Cheese

Prep Time: 2 Minutes
Cook Time: 10 Minutes   Serves: 1

Ingredients:

- 2 Slices of Crusty Bread
- 40 g Sliced or Grated Cheddar Cheese
- 10 g Margarine or Mayonnaise

Directions:

1. Take your bread, layer up the cheese.
2. Make into a sandwich.
3. Spread the outside (not inside!) with butter or mayonnaise.
4. Preheat the air fryer basket to 180°C for 1-2 minutes.
5. Cook for 10 minutes. Flip 5 minutes in.
6. Serve with your choice of crisps or even a nice simple salad to make it a little more balanced.

Nutritional Value (Amount per Serving):

Calories: 248; Fat: 12.9; Carb: 24.13; Protein: 8.93

Air Fryer Stuffing Balls

Prep Time: 2 Minutes
Cook Time: 15 Minutes   Serves: 4

Ingredients:

- 1 Slice Bread
- 1 Medium Onion
- 30ml Olive Oil
- 30g Unsalted Butter
- Small Handful Fresh Sage or 1 tbsp Dried Sage

Directions:

1. Combine together the olive oil and butter in a wide based frying pan and heat until melted completely. Stir well.
2. Chop the onion and add this in.
3. Cook until translucent, usually 2-3 minutes.
4. Chop or roughly rip the bread and add this in. Stir well and cook for 1-2 minutes.
5. Chop the sage and add this in. Cook for 1 minute.
6. Stir well.
7. Place your mix into a food processor and pulse together until it is a fine consistency.
8. Roll into balls and then you can place the balls into the air fryer basket. (I aim for small balls, as you can see from the pictures. These are an ideal serving size for everyone to enjoy a couple alongside their dinner.)
9. Cook in the air fryer at 200°C for 10 minutes. Gently shake the basket halfway through cooking

Nutritional Value (Amount per Serving):

Calories: 518; Fat: 47.56; Carb: 21.37; Protein: 4.18

Chapter 7: Fish and Seafood

Air Fryer Frozen Fish Fingers

Prep Time: 1 Minute
Cook Time: 8-11 Minutes   Serves: 10

Ingredients:

- 10 Frozen Fish Fingers

Directions:

1. Preheat air fryer for 2 or 3 minutes at 200°C.
2. Lay the frozen fish fingers in the air fryer basket.
3. Set the timer to 8 minutes.
4. Turn the fish fingers at 4 minutes.
5. The fish fingers should be crispy and golden on the outside and piping hot all the way through. If they are not, air fry them for a further 2 or 3 minutes.

Nutritional Value (Amount per Serving):

Calories: 184; Fat: 10.61; Carb: 0; Protein: 20.7

Honey-Glazed Salmon

Prep Time: 11 Minutes
Cook Time: 16 Minutes   Serves: 2

Ingredients:

- 6 tsp Gluten-Free Soy Sauce
- 2 Salmon Fillets
- 3 tsp Sweet Rice Wine
- 1 tsp Water   • 6 tbsp Honey

Directions:

1. In a bowl, mix sweet rice wine, soy sauce, honey, and water.
2. Set half of it aside.
3. Marinate the fish in the other half of the prepared marinade and let it rest for 2 hours.
4. Let the air fryer preheat to 180°C.
5. Cook the fish for 8 minutes, flip halfway through, and cook for another 5 minutes.
6. Baste the salmon with marinade mixture after 3 or 4 minutes.
7. Using the second half of the prepared marinade, pour into a saucepan,

reduce to half, serve the sauce with the fish.

Nutritional Value (Amount per Serving):

Calories: 1205; Fat: 30.62; Carb: 134.83; Protein: 94.05

Air Fryer Lemon Cod

Prep Time: 5 Minutes
Cook Time: 10 Minutes   Serves: 1

Ingredients:

- 1 Cod Fillet
- 1 tbsp Chopped Dried Parsley
- Kosher Salt and Pepper, to taste
- 1 tbsp Garlic Powder
- 1 Lemon, sliced

Directions:

1. Mix all ingredients, except the cod, in a bowl and use to coat the fish fillet.
2. Slice the lemon and lay it at the bottom of the air fryer basket.
3. Put spiced fish on top of the lemon slices. Cover the fish with lemon slices.
4. Cook for 10 minutes at 190°C, the internal temperature of fish should be 65°C.
5. Serve.

Nutritional Value (Amount per Serving):

Calories: 142; Fat: 0.78; Carb: 14.86; Protein: 20.5

Air Fryer Courgette Crisps

Prep Time: 30 Minutes
Cook Time: 30 Minutes   Serves: 2

Ingredients:

- 2 Courgettes, sliced into a 1/8-inch thick discs
- Pinch Sea Salt
- White Pepper, to taste
- 1 tbsp Olive Oil, for drizzling

Directions:

1. Preheat the air fryer to 165°C.
2. Put courgettes in a bowl with salt. Let it

sit in a colander to drain for 30 minutes.
3. Layer courgettes in a baking dish. Drizzle with oil. Season with pepper. Place baking dish in the air fryer basket. Cook for 30 minutes.
4. Adjust seasoning. Serve.

Nutritional Value (Amount per Serving):

Calories: 71; Fat: 6.89; Carb: 2.47; Protein: 0.75

Air Fryer Shrimp Recipe (Fresh or Frozen)

Prep Time: 10 Minutes
Cook Time: 8 Minutes   Serves: 4

Ingredients:

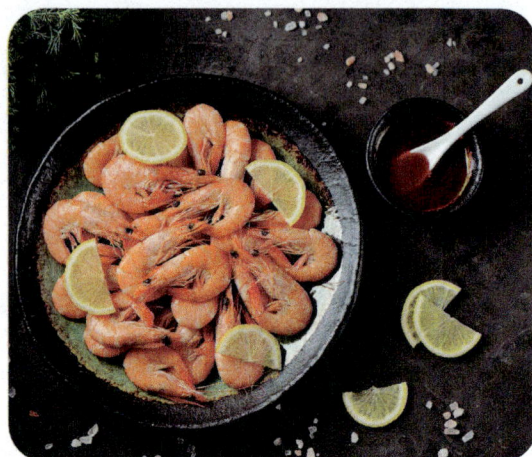

- 450 g Shrimps: frozen, thawed or fresh
- 1 Large Fresh Garlic Clove, minced (substitute with garlic powder if desired)
- 30 g Unsalted Butter, cut into small cubes
- Salt and Pepper to taste
- Cooking Oil Spray
- ½ Lemon, juice
- 1 tbsp Parsley, chopped to garnish.

Directions:

1. Clean and devein the shrimps (deshell if desired).
2. Transfer the shrimps to an oven safe dish that fits into your air fryer basket
3. Season shrimps with salt and pepper, spray with a little cooking oil and stir to combine. Add butter cubes to the shrimps then place the dish in the air fryer basket.
4. Cook for 8 to 10 minutes on 200°C. There is no need to flip the shrimp halfway through but I do this for good measure.
5. Remove from the air fryer, add some chopped parsley and squeeze some lemon juice on the shrimps if desired. Stir to combine. Serve and enjoy!

Nutritional Value (Amount per Serving):

Calories: 213; Fat: 12.31; Carb: 17.03; Protein: 9.42

Easy Air Fryer Cod

Prep Time: 5 Minutes
Cook Time: 10 Minutes   Serves: 4

Ingredients:

- 4 x 125g Fresh Cod Loins (you can substitute for fillets too)
- 30 g Melted Unsalted Butter
- 1 Lemon, sliced   • Salt to taste
- Black Pepper to taste

Directions:

1. Preheat the air fryer to 200°C for 5 minutes.
2. Pat the cod loins or fillets dry so they are moisture free. Season the fish generously with salt and black pepper then brush the melted butter on one side of the fish
3. Spray the air fryer basket with cooking oil. Place the cod loins/fillets in the air fryer basket buttered side down making sure they are not touching. Brush the remaining butter on top of the fish, add one lemon slice to each of the fish
4. Cook for 10 minutes, carefully remove the fish and transfer to a plate.
5. Serve with lemon butter sauce, roasted potatoes and vegetables.

Nutritional Value (Amount per Serving):

Calories: 407; Fat: 26.68; Carb: 13.14; Protein: 29.26

Fishcakes Two Ways

Prep Time: 20 Minutes
Cook Time: 6 Minutes   Serves: 1

Ingredients:

- 600g Potatoes • 2 Garlic Cloves
- 8g Parsley • 70g Capers
- 4g Dill • Zest of 2 Lemons
- 1 tsp Salt • 1/2 tsp Pepper
- 45g Mayonnaise (use vegan friendly if following a vegan diet)

For the Coating:
- 130g Flour
- 130g Toasted Breadcrumbs

- 45g cup Mayonnaise (or use vegan friendly as above)

For the Salmon Fish Cakes:
- 210g Tinned Skinless and Boneless Salmon

For the Jackfruit Fishcakes:
- 565g tin Jackfruit
- 3-5g Nori Chips Plain or Salt Flavoured (added to your taste)

Optional Serving Suggestion:
- Mayonnaise or Tartare Sauce (use vegan friendly as above)
- Green Salad of Peas, Rocket, and more Pickled Dill
- Lemon Wedges

Directions:

1. Peel the potatoes and cut into roughly 5cm chunks.
2. Place into a saucepan and cover with water, and bring to the boil. Cook until soft enough to mash.
3. While the potatoes boil, prepare your ingredients. Pick the fennel or dill fronds and parsley from any thicker stems and chop finely, then finely grate the garlic, and combine all in a bowl. Zest two lemons and add to the bowl, reserving the remaining lemon for serving.
4. Drain the jackfruit and place the flesh into a bowl of freshwater until needed. Also drain the salmon and place into a bowl.
5. Once the potatoes are cooked, mash them until smooth and add them to the bowl with the chopped herbs, capers, lemon zest, and garlic. Season with salt and pepper. Lightly stir the mixture together, then stir in the mayonnaise and mix until just combined.
6. Divide the fishcake base in to two separate bowls and add the salmon to one half, and the jackfruit and crispy nori to the other.
7. Mix each bowl until just combined, then divide each mix into 4 and shape into fish cakes.
8. Prepare for dredging by putting the toasted breadcrumbs in one dish, the flour in another and the mayo mixed with a little water into a third.
9. Dip your fishcakes into the flour, then into the thinned mayo and finally into the breadcrumbs - making sure to lightly press the crumbs into the fish cake.
10. Place your fishcakes into your air fryer – with the salmon fishcakes in one batch and the jackfruit fishcakes in another. Lightly spritz the fishcakes with olive oil spray whilst in the basket.
11. Select set the temperature to 200°C and set the time for 6 minutes.
12. Halfway through cooking flip the fishcakes.
13. Once cooked, serve the fishcakes, alongside a salad, some more mayonnaise or tartare sauce and lemon wedges.

Nutritional Value (Amount per Serving):

Calories: 797; Fat: 27.99; Carb: 110.45; Protein: 34.31

Rice Paper Rolls

Prep Time: 10 Minutes
Cook Time: 11 Minutes   Serves: 1

Ingredients:

- 1 Onion, halved and thinly sliced
- 4 Medium Carrots, peeled and julienned
- 150g Cabbage, thinly sliced
- 4 Cloves Garlic, grated
- 5cm Piece Ginger, grated
- 4 Spring Onions, thinly sliced
- 1 tsp Miso Paste (optional)
- 1 tbsp Cornflour
- 1 Chicken Breast, cooked and shredded
- 300g Chopped and Sautéed Mushrooms
- 1 tsp Lao Gan Ma Chilli Crisp, optional
- 16 Rice Paper Wrappers
- 2 tsp Sesame Oil, for brushing

Directions:

1. Add 1 tbsp oil to a wok and stir fry the onions and carrots until starting to soften then add the cabbage, garlic and ginger.
2. Remove the wok from the heat, then add the spring onions and miso.
3. Sieve over the cornflour and stir everything together. Season to taste with salt.
4. Divide the mixture into two. To one add the cooked shredded chicken, and to the other half add the mushrooms and chilli crisp. Mix each flavour to combine.
5. Make the crispy rice dumplings by dipping the rice paper wrapper into some warm water until coated, then lay it on a clean dry surface. Once it has softened and is pliable, add a few tablespoons of filling to the top quarter of the wrapper. Fold the left and right sides of the wrapper in then roll the parcels together. Add another wrapper around the parcel, to create a double layer of rice paper. Then repeat the process for the remaining filling.
6. Brush the parcels with sesame oil, and place in the air fryer, with the mushroom parcels in one batch and the chicken in another.
7. Air fry at 205°C and set the time for 11 minutes.
8. Flip the rice paper parcels over at halfway point.
9. Once cooked, serve the crispy rice paper parcels with your choice of dipping sauce.

Nutritional Value (Amount per Serving):

Calories: 766; Fat: 35.5; Carb: 79.54; Protein: 41.53

Chapter 8: Desserts

Air Fryer Apricot and Raisin Cake

Prep Time: 10 Minutes
Cook Time: 10-15 Minutes   Serves: 8

Ingredients:

- 75g Dried Apricots
- 4 tbsp Orange Juice
- 75g Self-Raising Flour   • 40g Sugar
- 1 Egg   • 75g Raisins

Directions:

1. Preheat air fryer to 160°C.
2. In a blender or food processor blend the dried apricots and orange juice until they are smooth.
3. In a separate bowl, mix together the sugar and flour.
4. Beat the egg. Add it to the flour and sugar. Mix together.
5. Add the apricot puree and raisins. Combine together.
6. Spray an air fryer safe baking tin with a little oil. Transfer the mixture to the baking tin and level off.
7. Cook in the air fryer for 12 minutes, check it at 10 minutes. Use a metal skewer to see if it is done. If need be, return the cake to the air fryer to cook for a few more minutes to brown up.
8. Allow to cool before removing from the baking tin and slicing up.

Nutritional Value (Amount per Serving):

Calories: 95; Fat: 1.37; Carb: 18.8; Protein: 2.58

Air Fryer Carrot Cake

Prep Time: 10 Minutes
Cook Time: 25-30 Minutes   Serves: 1

Ingredients:

- 140g Soft Brown Sugar
- 2 Eggs, beaten   • 140g Butter
- 1 Orange, zest and juice
- 200g Self-Raising Flour
- 1tsp Ground Cinnamon
- 175g Grated Carrot, (approx 2 medium carrots)   • 60g Sultanas

Directions:

1. Preheat air fryer to 175°C.
2. In a bowl, cream together the butter and sugar.
3. Slowly add the beaten eggs.
4. Fold in the flour, a little bit at a time, mixing it as you go. Add the orange juice and zest, grated carrots, cinnamon and sultanas. Gently mix all the ingredients together.
5. Grease the baking tin and pour the mixture in.
6. Place baking tin in the air fryer basket and cook for 25-30 minutes. Check to see if the cake is cooked using a cocktail stick or metal skewer. If it comes out wet, then cook it for a little longer.
7. Remove the baking tin from the air fryer basket and allow to cool for 10 minutes before removing from the tin.

Nutritional Value (Amount per Serving):

Calories: 2647; Fat: 135.17; Carb: 314.17; Protein: 41.41

Air Fryer Rhubarb Crumble

Prep Time: 5 Minutes
Cook Time: 15 Minutes   Serves: 4

Ingredients:

For the Filling:
- 150 g White Sugar
- 20 g Plain Flour
- 1/2 tsp Vanilla Extract
- 500 g Rhubarb
- Spray Oil or Butter, to grease ramekins

For the Topping:
- 120 g Plain Flour
- 80 g Cold Butter, cut into cubes
- 1/8 tsp Salt
- 60 g Light Brown Sugar

Directions:

1. Preheat the air fryer to 190°C.
2. In a large mixing bowl, combine together the white sugar, plain flour and vanilla extract.
3. Wash the rhubarb and remove the ends. Cut into 1/2 inch pieces.
4. Add the rhubarb to your filling mixture and stir well
5. Place into the lightly greased ramekins.
6. Combine the flour and butter, it is a crumble consistency.
7. Add the salt and brown sugar and mix well.
8. Place this over the top of your filling.
9. Bake at 190°C for 15 minutes.

10. Serve with lashings of custard and enjoy!

Nutritional Value (Amount per Serving):

Calories: 775; Fat: 22.74; Carb: 118.16; Protein: 29.14

Air Fryer Chocolate Brownies

Prep Time: 10 Minutes
Cook Time: 20-25 Minutes   Serves: 16

Ingredients:

- 1 Pack Brownie Mix
- 3 tbsp Vegetable Oil
- 75ml Water
- 1 Medium Egg

Directions:

1. Pour the brownie mix into a bowl then add the water, vegetable oil and egg. Mix it thoroughly and ensure the mixture doesn't have any lumps.
2. Grease an air fryer baking tin and spread the mixture evenly, with a spatula.
3. Set the air fryer to 160°C and let the brownies cook for 20-25 minutes. Stick a knife into the brownie and if it comes out almost clean the brownies should be cooked.
4. Allow to cool then slice into squares and enjoy your air fried brownies.

Nutritional Value (Amount per Serving):

Calories: 204; Fat: 9.44; Carb: 29.74; Protein: 2.13

Air Fryer Fruit Scones

Prep Time: 5 Minutes
Cook Time: 8-10 Minutes   Serves: 4

Ingredients:

- 120g Self-Raising Flour (use 5g more flour for scones that can be cut with a cutter)
- A Pinch of Salt
- 40g Butter
- 20g Sultanas

- 20g Sugar
- 75ml Semi-Skimmed Milk

Directions:

1. Preheat your air fryer, if needed, to 200°C.
2. Mix flour and butter together until you have a breadcrumb-like consistency. Add a pinch of salt.
3. Mix in the sultanas. Then stir in the sugar.
4. Add milk and mix
5. Divide into 4.
6. Line your air fryer basket with parchment paper.
7. Drop the mixture in. You can either go for drop scones or you can just add 5g more flour for a dryer consistency (if needed) and use a cutter.
8. Cook for 8-10 minutes at 200°C. Use a cake tester to ensure they're cooked through before serving.

Nutritional Value (Amount per Serving):

Calories: 1014; Fat: 54.4; Carb: 61.1; Protein: 69.41

Air Fryer Cookies

Prep Time: 10 Minutes
Cook Time: 5 Minutes   Serves: 24

Ingredients:

- 135g Salted Butter
- 70g Light Brown Sugar
- 70g Caster Sugar
- 10ml Vanilla Extract
- 1 Medium Egg
- 225g Plain Flour
- 1/2 tsp Bicarbonate of Soda
- Pinch of Salt
- 175g Chocolate Chunks or Chips
- Spray Oil

Directions:

1. Beat the butter and both sugars together in a bowl.
2. Once mixed, add the egg and vanilla extract.
3. In a separate bowl, combine the flour, bicarbonate of soda, salt and chocolate chunks (or chips).
4. Add the dry ingredients to the wet ingredients and mix until combined well.

5. Roll the dough into a long sausage shape and chill for a minimum of 1 hour. This will help to make a more deliciously chewy cookie. (Occasionally I've left the dough overnight and the cookies are even better!)

6. Remove the dough from the fridge.

7. Roll out the cookie dough. (I've experimented with balls, lightly press down with a fork, moulding cookie shapes and just cutting off a little slab from the chilled dough and they all take very similar time to cook, with similar results, so just be lazy and cut a slab off if you fancy!)

8. Preheat the air fryer to 180°C for 1-2 minutes if required.

9. Cut a piece of parchment paper to fit the bottom of your air fryer. (Without this the cookie dough may mould to the shape of the bottom of your basket and it will be a nightmare to get it off without breaking the cookie).

10. Lightly spray the parchment paper with spray oil

11. Cook in the air fryer for 5 minutes.

12. Transfer to a wire cooling rack, still on the parchment paper, and leave to cool for 5 minutes.

13. Gently peel back the parchment paper and you can enjoy your cookies while they are still warm, or they'll keep for 2-3 days in an airtight container.

Nutritional Value (Amount per Serving):

Calories: 174; Fat: 6.98; Carb: 19.54; Protein: 1.6

Air Fryer Pizookie

Prep Time: 5 Minutes
Cook Time: 5 Minutes   Serves: 8

Ingredients:

- 135g Salted Butter, at room temperature
- 70g Light Brown Sugar
- 70g Caster Sugar
- 10ml Vanilla Extract
- 1 Egg
- 225g Plain Flour
- 1/2 tsp Bicarbonate of Soda
- 175g Chocolate Chunks or Chocolate Chips

Directions:

1. Combine the butter and both sugars in a bowl.
2. Add the egg and vanilla extract once combined.
3. In a separate bowl, mix together the flour, bicarbonate of soda and

chocolate chunks/chocolate chips.

4. Combine the wet and dry ingredients in a bowl and mix until just combined.

5. Once the dough is mixed roll it out into a circular shape, wrap in clingfilm and then chill for a minimum of 1 hour. (or overnight if you'd prefer). Chilling helps make a chewier, more delicious cookie.

6. Add the dry ingredients to the wet ingredients and mix until combined well.

7. I like to make either 4 mini pizookies with this dough or one large one that will serve 8 people comfortably.

8. Take your chilled cookie dough ou of the fridge, roll it out and then shape it to fit either a cake pan or a cast iron skillet which gives a great result with a chewy cookie with a well-cooked bottom.

9. Preheat the air fryer to 180°C for 1-2 minutes

10. Add the skillet, cake pan, or even just the dough to a baking paper lined air fryer basket, and then cook for 5 minutes at 180°C.

11. Remove from the air fryer and then transfer to a wire cooling rack to cool down.

12. If you used parchment paper, gently peel this back once the cookie has cooled slightly and it'll keep for 2-3 days.

Nutritional Value (Amount per Serving):

Calories: 531; Fat: 21.62; Carb: 58.7; Protein: 5.23

Air Fryer Peanut Butter Cookies

Prep Time: 4 Minutes
Cook Time: 4-6 Minutes   Serves: 20

Ingredients:

- 250g Smooth Peanut Butter
- 250g White Caster Sugar
- 1 Egg

Directions:

1. Mix together all the ingredients to a smooth consistency. Try not to overwork the mixture.

2. Line your air fryer basket with baking paper. (You can use reusable baking paper if you have this).

3. (If you're going to make multiple batches like I do then you'll want to measure the baking paper before you heat up the air fryer, cut your paper and then you'll have it all to hand ready to line the basket before adding the

cookie dough).

4. Place walnut sized balls of the dough on to the baking paper.
5. Press down lightly with a fork or spoon, depending on whether you want the little cut indentations or not.
6. Cook at 200°C for 4 minutes. Check at the 2-minute mark just to ensure the dough balls haven't moved together as air flow can be very strong in some air fryer models.
7. Remove from the oven when they are just lightly golden brown to avoid burning them.
8. Depending on your air fryer model you may want to add another 1-2 minutes of cook time.
9. Remove from the air fryer basket and leave to cool on a wire rack. Remove the parchment paper, carefully, using a spatula if necessary, and then transfer to a wire rack.

Nutritional Value (Amount per Serving):

Calories: 109; Fat: 8.58; Carb: 6.79; Protein: 2.15

CONCLUSION

An air fryer is one of the most versatile cooking appliances, and it can be used to cook a variety of foods in single cooking appliance. It allows you to air fry, roast, bake, grill, reheat, and dehydrate your favourite food. One of the best reasons to use an air fryer is it requires much less fat/oil to cook your food.

This cookbook contains healthy and delicious air fryer recipes which include breakfasts to desserts. The recipes in this cookbook are unique and healthy. Each recipe starts with the preparation and cooking times followed by an ingredients list and step-by-step cooking instructions. All the recipes end with their nutritional value information, to help you to keep track of your daily calorie consumption.

APPENDIX RECIPE INDEX

Printed in Great Britain
by Amazon